The House as Witness

poems by Veronica Tucker

QUILLKEEPERS PRESS

ISBN: 978-1-969601-01-9

Published by Quillkeepers Press, LLC
PO Box 10236
Casa Grande, AZ 85130

For this house in New Hampshire,
which held our lives quietly
and without judgment.

For my parents, who taught me
that a home is made through
care and time.

For Bill, who filled these rooms
with steadiness and laughter.

For Olivia, Felicity, and William,
whose footsteps and voices
made this house alive.

Section I:
Foundations

Blueprint Breathes

The house was lines on paper

before it was walls.

Ink translated into beams,

measurements into air.

We stood in the empty lot,

picturing where voices would rise,

where laughter would catch in stairwells,

where quiet would pool like dust.

The blueprint exhaled slowly,

waiting for us to fill it.

Every square became a possibility,

each rectangle a promise.

I thought of how bones hold the body upright,

how the body makes space for a heart.

The house was not yet ours.

Still, it breathed.

When the Walls First Listened

On the first night,we said little.

Boxes stacked like silent witnesses,

windows without curtains.

The refrigerator hummed louder than sleep,

and every step echoed back

as if the house were testing us.

I whispered a child's name

and the plaster seemed to lean closer.

I opened a book

and the pages crackled too loudly,

their voices ricocheting off bare walls.

It felt like we had moved

into something alive,

and it had been waiting to hear.

Keys in the Lock

The keys were heavier
than I expected,
as if metal carried memory.
They turned reluctantly,
like the house tested our belonging.

Behind the door,
lay air

that had not yet learned our scent,
rooms unclaimed by laughter or grief.
We stepped in together,
hands carrying groceries and toys,
feet tracking dirt from other lives.
The door clicked shut.

That sound will repeat
again and again,
marking every entry, every leaving,
long after we are gone.

First Night, Empty Rooms

We unrolled two sleeping bags

on the hardwood that still smelled like trees.

The children whispered into the ceiling,

their syllables drifting like moths.

No curtains yet,

only the moon testing the glass,

the streetlamp tracing our corner of floor.

I listened for the house

introducing itself.

Pipes cleared their throats.

The heater exhaled once, then again.

A plank answered footsteps

with its own memory.

The hallway held its breath.

The closets waited without judgment.

In the smallest room I could hear

the shape of a crib not yet assembled,

a chair not yet placed

for late nights

that would try to swallow me.

Sleep came slowly,

a visitor at the knob.

Even without furniture, the house

found ways to hold us.

Nail by Nail, We Entered

We carried our lives in cardboard,

inked labels that were both true and not.

Kitchen. Books. Winter things.

No box for hope,

so we tucked it into all the others.

The hammer gave its rhythm.

The walls accepted small silver commas

that became frames.

We made shelves of pine,

sanded until the grain felt like voice.

A door dragged, then lifted.

The stair rail asked for a hand

and I gave mine.

The children scattered.

One closet became a fort.

Another held dust motes

rising like tiny suns.

We ate on the floor that first week,

pizza on a towel,

paper cups with names in marker.

By evening the walls had more to say.

They held photographs that proved we existed

before the address knew us.

We entered by building,

by asking permission,

listening to the answer rise through wood.

The Sound of Settling

After a week the house began to speak

in a language I almost understood.

A low click beneath the window at dusk.

A soft tic along the baseboard when the day cooled.

Joists shifting their long shoulders.

The floor offering a sigh

where the hallway meets the stairs.

I learned what was nothing to fear.

Wind rehearsing in the eaves.

The fridge with its choir of small throats.

Even the roof with its cedar patience

answering heat with release.

Not ghosts,

only physics with a heartbeat.

We settled too.

Shoes found the tray by the door.

Mail learned the bowl beside the keys.

Morning coffee traced its path

from kettle to cup to window.

The children measured themselves

against the pantry door.

Sometimes at night the house was louder,

as if remembering its trees,

as if the nails dreamed of leaving.

I would wake and listen,

let the noise pass through.

There is music to belonging.

What once startled,

becomes a lullaby.

Threshold Step

There is always a small ceremony at the door,
even when hands are full and the day is loud.
The mat receives what the world has tried to keep on us.
Mud becomes story. Sand becomes summer.
Snow becomes the breath of a field
that followed us home.

Inside, the air lifts differently.
The house steps with us,
matching the pace of shoulders that finally lower.
I pause in the rectangle of entry,
let the outside fall from my cuffs,
let the inside rise to meet my chest.

Children rush past like tides
that have memorized the moon.
Dogs circle, inhale, decide it is safe again.
I hang a coat and feel the stitch of routine hold.
The door closes and draws a line.
Each return writes a promise on the woodweave.
We will come back. We will keep coming back.
Every step writes us here,
until it doesn't.

Section II:
Rooms of Becoming

The Kitchen Holds the Center

Every road in the house ends here.

Counters catch the day's debris,

keys beside an apple core,

a permission slip curling at its edge.

The stove warms without asking,

its hum steady as breath.

Children orbit in and out,

their questions trailing like satellites.

The fridge door opens wide

as if it were a book of need,

revealing half a jug of milk,

a jar of mustard without a lid.

Here voices rise together,

layered and imperfect,

a choir of ordinary survival.

Even arguments find their way

to this room,

where they dissolve

under the click of silverware

and the slow steam of pasta water.

At night, the table becomes still.

A single glass waits for morning.

Even in quiet,

the kitchen holds the center,

a lantern against the dark.

Crayon Marks Beneath the Paint

I tried to cover them once,

rolling beige over the wild arcs of color.

But the wall remembers.

When afternoon sun leans hard,

shapes glow through like ghosts.

The children had drawn entire worlds,

blue rivers without banks,

stars without symmetry,

faces that smiled without reason.

They pressed crayons so hard

that wax still ridges the wall.

I think of the small hands,

their urgency to leave a mark.

Laughter rose like wind behind them,

a storm that refused instruction.

I wanted to keep the walls clean,

but the walls wanted a story.

Now I leave them as they are,

buried but breathing,

a secret between plaster and light.

Paint cannot undo joy.

It only teaches it how to hide,

waiting for someone patient enough

to notice.

Upstairs Light at 3 A.M.

The hallway bulb is too bright

for the hour,

yet it burns anyway,

casting yellow across the carpet

like a false sun.

I step carefully,

past doors where

breathing steadies

into small oceans.

The light follows,

silent but insistent,

marking me as both watcher

and watched.

Sometimes a cry wakes me,

sharp as broken glass.

Other nights it is nothing more

than my own unease,

the body remembering

that sleep is fragile.

I have crossed this hall

with a thermometer in one hand,

a storybook in the other.

I have carried a fevered child,

their heat soaking my shoulder

until I could no longer tell

where they ended,

where I began.

The bulb flickers once

but does not go out.

Neither do I.

Laundry Spinning Like Time

The washer begins its slow whirl,

a tide gathering its rhythm.

Shirts collapse into one another,

socks turn reckless cartwheels.

The sound repeats weekly,

then daily,

then without end.

Foam climbs the glass

like seasons rising and fading.

I fold what returns to me,

crease by crease,

as if control could be pressed into cloth.

Still, stains hold fast,

and one sleeve carries the ghost of a cough.

The basket grows heavy

but never full enough to finish.

I carry it upstairs like an offering,

lay shirts in neat stacks

that topple as soon as they are claimed.

Time spins, then drains.

I load it again.

What else can I do

but honor the ritual

of what is always unfinished?

The Hall Closet's Secrets

Behind the door

are scarves that no one wears,

a box of gloves that never match.

Shelves bend under the weight of things

we meant to need.

Here lives the umbrella

that failed us in rain,

the winter boots two sizes too small.

Every closet is a museum

of mistakes and intentions.

If you listen long enough

you can hear the objects whisper,

not anger, only reminder:

We were chosen once.

We were carried here with hope.

Sometimes I open it,

just to stand inside.

The smell of dust and cedar

wraps around me like a

half-remembered coat.

The house keeps our secrets

even when we've forgotten them.

It waits for the day

we open the door again,

bracing ourselves to decide

what to keep,

what to let go.

Basement of Forgotten Boxes

The basement smells of stone and iron,
the kind of damp that softens cardboard.
Labels fade,
but the boxes know their names.

I crouch among them,
lifting lids to half-lives:
college notebooks,
a wedding dress folded like silence,
toys missing pieces of themselves.
Spiders string patient webs across corners,
each thread more honest
than the promises stored here.
A child's bike frame rusts slowly,
its wheels frozen mid-turn.

When I close the lids,
the boxes sigh in relief.
They know I will not stay long.
I flick the light and climb the stairs,
leaving the basement to hold
what I am not ready to release.

Game Room Over the Garage

Laughter echoes differently here,
bouncing against the sloped ceiling.
The floor remembers every step of chase,
every dropped card,
every slam of a door too late.

The television hums in one corner,
controllers tangled like snakes.
A dartboard holds more holes than wins.
The carpet is worn thin
where someone once danced alone.

This room belongs to a season of noise,
when children grow faster than rules,
when every sound feels urgent.
I know one day it will empty itself,
wait for a new weight,
echo more softly.

For now, it is wild with presence,
a room louder than memory,
a room that refuses to be forgotten.

The Children's Voices Carry Through Vents

From the kitchen I hear them upstairs,

not the words but the rise and fall.

Their voices slip into the vents,

traveling through hidden passages

like messengers between worlds.

Arguments arrive as sharp bursts.

Laughter spreads wide as a song.

Even silence has weight,

a pause

  that lands on the counter beside me.

The vents deliver everything,

whether I ask or not.

Some days it feels like intrusion,

a reminder that privacy

is thin as plaster.

Other days it is comfort,

proof they are near

even when the house folds us apart.

The ducts hold their music,

carry it from one room to another,

until it reaches me like prayer.

The house does not let me forget

I am part of the chorus,

even when I want quiet.

Section III:

The Apartment at the Back of the House

Curtains Drawn Quietly

Her curtains never swung wide.

Light was measured in strips,

slanted through fabric heavy with dust.

Privacy was her first prayer,

silence her second.

From the hallway I caught

the faint outline of her chair,

her hand tracing the armrest

like a map she knew by heart.

The curtains breathed

only when the window was cracked,

a slow pulse of air

no one else noticed.

I wonder now if she drew them

to keep us out

or to keep herself in,

the fabric a border

between presence and retreat.

Even the house lowered its voice

as it passed her door.

The dog slowed there too,

nosing the crack beneath the frame,

waiting for a signal

that never came.

When the curtains finally stayed closed,

the window forgot the sun.

Still the fabric hung heavy,

as though guarding the last

of her shadow.

The Hallway Between Us

The apartment was just steps away,

but the hallway stretched longer

each year she grew smaller.

I carried trays of food,

a glass of water,

sometimes nothing at all

except the weight of being daughter.

Her door opened slow,

hinges aching with her.

She smiled at me with effort,

as though joy were a language

she had not spoken in years.

I lingered in the hallway,

unsure whether to cross the threshold.

Love can live in distance.

Sometimes it has to.

I thought of the years before,

when her stride was quick,

when she leaned in to whisper

secrets meant only for me.

Now she leaned back,

resting against her doorframe

like a shoreline giving way to tide.

I stood in the hallway

longer than I should have,

listening to the silence stretch

between her breath and mine.

Tea Cups Left in the Sink

She loved her tea strong,

leaves settled thick at the bottom.

I found cups in her sink,

rings of brown circling like time.

Each cup held its own confession:

a half-drunk morning,

an afternoon abandoned mid-sip,

an evening she tried to finish

but could not.

I washed them slowly,

fingers tracing porcelain

as though I could read her silence.

The house carried the scent of tea

longer than she did,

steam rising from a place

that had gone still.

Sometimes I left one cup

exactly where she had set it,

a small rebellion against absence.

The ring hardened day by day,

until I rinsed it away,

watching the circle vanish,

knowing memory does not.

Breath Slowed Inside These Walls

The house learned her rhythm first.

Not steady.

Not sharp.

Drawn out like fabric tearing.

At night I heard her through plaster,

inhalations caught mid-climb,

exhalations that barely made it.

Even the radiator hushed itself,

as if listening.

I sat outside her door.

Counted seconds.

One. Two.

Waited for air to return.

My own chest mirrored hers,

a borrowed struggle.

Every gasp a message

I could not answer.

The walls kept her secret.

They knew the truth

longer than I could hold it.

Breath

Slowed

Inside

These

walls.

Until the silence

was heavier

than sound.

A Television Left On Low

Her room glowed blue at night,

a screen murmuring reruns

she no longer followed.

The volume was low,

just enough to mimic company.

I stood in the doorway once,

watched the light play across her cheek.

Eyes closed, lips parted,

she looked like someone

listening to another world.

The television filled the silence

we could not.

Commercials for miracle cures,

sitcoms that had outlived their laughter.

She clutched the remote

as if it were a hand,

something solid to keep her tethered.

The house absorbed it all,

static woven into its beams.

Even after the screen went dark

I could hear its echo,

low voices still circling the air.

When she was gone,

I turned the television off.

The room was too quiet.

Even the house seemed surprised.

An Empty Chair in the Window

After she left,

the chair remained by the window,

fabric indented where her body leaned.

The sunlight still arrived each morning,

laying itself across the cushion

as though she might return to claim it.

Birds gathered at the feeder,

confused by the absence of hands

that once scattered seed.

I passed the doorway carefully,

unable to move the chair.

It was less furniture now,

more monument.

The house guarded it

like a relic,

refusing to let dust settle too quickly.

Even cobwebs avoided the legs,

as though respecting

what lingered there.

After she left,

One afternoon I sat in it myself,

waiting for the room to release her.

But the chair held me loosely,

like someone else's memory.

Her Door Closed,
the House Leaned In

We shut the door softly,

but the house felt it anyway.

Every board seemed to tilt

toward the absence,

every stair whispered her name.

The apartment no longer hummed.

Even the clock ticked quieter,

as if afraid to intrude.

Her belongings lingered in drawers,

small anchors that refused release.

The door stayed closed for weeks.

We walked past,

holding our breath.

It felt like the house itself

leaned against the frame,

listening for her

long after she was gone.

At night, I swear I heard her cough,

a sound caught in the grain of the wood.

The handle gleamed as if touched,

though no one entered.

The house leaned in.

The house remembered.

The house refused

to let her absence be silent.

Section IV:
Seasons

Maple Leaves Against the Siding

They arrive like soft hands,

pressing the house with color.

Red warms the clapboard,

gold writes small fires across the wall.

The siding accepts every touch

without complaint.

Children rake by the steps,

then leap into their own work,

leaves breaking into laughter beneath them.

A glove falls from a pocket,

waits in the grass like a patient animal.

The house breathes sap and earth.

Windows turn into frames for the yard,

each pane a smaller season.

Inside, mugs find our palms,

fogging the glass in brief circles

that vanish and return.

Maples lean close,

confiding what they know about letting go.

They press their bright foreheads to the house

until the color rubs off on us.

By evening the gutters are full,

a quiet river of what has already fallen.

We sweep the steps.

We make room for what comes next.

The house keeps a few leaves tucked

where the wind cannot reach,

as if to hold a last warm touch

through the colder voice of the year.

And we watch the trees strip themselves bare,

reminding us that beauty

was never meant to last unchanged.

Snow on the Roofline

The first snow writes a soft sentence

across the roof,

each shingle translated into hush.

The yard erases itself,

fenceposts turning into dim shoulders,

paths into memory.

We listen to the sky lower,

thick and deliberate.

Pine boughs bow until they find

their quieter truth.

The chimney releases a thin column

that fades into cloud like a secret returned.

Inside, floors pick up the creak of boots,

mats darken with thaw.

Coats bloom along the hooks,

an orchard of wool and salt.

Children pull curtains open

to watch flakes fatten in the porch light,

counting until numbers fail.

The roofline settles into its winter weight,

shoulders squared to the long work.

It learns to carry this pale burden

without complaint.

At night the house expands a fraction,

wood responding to cold with its own slow voice.

We sleep while the storm keeps writing.

By morning the sentence has lengthened,

clean and unbroken.

The roofline waits for our boots to arrive,

to carve the first word of thaw

into its wide white page.

Winter Draft at the Doorframe

There is a seam the weather finds

no matter how carefully we seal it.

Cold fingers the threshold,

slides thin as breath along the floor,

finds the ankles of anyone waiting there.

I roll a towel and press it to the crack.

The house approves with a soft click.

Still the draft writes its name

along the baseboard,

a script you feel more than see.

Shoes gather on the mat like a small crowd.

Scarves nest in a basket that never empties.

We learn to greet the chill like a guest,

short visits, brief complaints,

then deeper

into the rooms where the heat holds.

Some evenings I stand in the doorway,

let a little winter enter my lungs.

It tastes like metal and pine,

a narrow brightness that wakes the tongue.

The door closes,

but not for long.

Weather knows every weakness we keep.

The house and I share a look,

choosing to forgive one more time.

Spring at the Edge of the Yard

Snow loosens its hold,

retreats into shadowed corners

like a shy animal.

The first green is not a color

but a promise,

a wet sheen along the ditch

where meltwater learns to speak.

At the edge of the yard,

mud receives our boots without judgment.

Worms sew the ground back together.

Pine pollen dusts the steps,

a yellow letter from trees

that never learned restraint.

We find last year's toys

where the grass kept them safe,

a small shovel, a faded ball,

plastic rings that remember the game.

The basement window opens

for the first time in months,

breathing out a winter kept in jars.

Inside, we put away the heaviest coats
but keep them close,
because spring in this place
is both invitation and dare.
The house smells like rain
even before it falls,
boards swelling with the memory
of rivers under bark.

At dusk, peepers begin their thin music.
The children press faces to the screen,
counting a sound you cannot count.
We stand at the edge of the yard
and feel the earth stand up,
slowly, surely,
glad for our weight again.

The season opens the door,
but only for those who remember
to step gently back into its arms.

Summer on the Deck

Evening lays itself across the boards,

warm and familiar.

The grill ticks as it cools,

a small language of satisfaction.

Cups gather rings on the rail,

lemon seeds drying into tiny moons.

We eat outside when the wind allows it,

napkins pinched beneath forks,

stories lifted by a gentle breeze.

The dogs patrol the perimeter,

tails writing bright cursive in the air.

Somewhere a neighbor laughs

and the laugh becomes ours for a moment.

The house opens all its windows,

screens humming with moths and hope.

Music drifts from the kitchen

to the deck and back again.

Bare feet learn the soft splinters

that insist on attention.

The yard invites one more game.

The sky holds the ball longer than it should.

We linger after the plates are cleared,

talk thinning into the kind of silence

that means enough has been said.

By night, the deck cools to slate.

Stars show up late

but stay until we notice them.

We carry candles inside,

hands cupped around their small weather,

and close the door gently

so the summer does not spill out too quickly.

Tomorrow the sun will rise earlier than we want,

but tonight we let it set as slowly as possible.

Rain Through the Screened Porch

The porch becomes a drumhead,

each drop a fingertip.

Rain threads itself through the screens

and hangs there like beads,

rows of clear prayer.

We sit in wicker that remembers other storms,

cushions darkening by degrees.

The air smells like coins and clover.

Thunder travels the slower road,

arriving when it wants,

never in a hurry to explain itself.

Children count between flash and sound,

negotiating with distance.

The dog refuses the outer step,

chooses instead the exact center of the rug,

where water cannot reach.

Inside, someone leaves a book open,

pages lifting in the damp
like wings that are almost ready.
The house relaxes into the weather,
wood taking what it needs,
releasing what it does not.

When the storm thins,
the porch gleams.
Screens jeweled with the last small drops,
each one a world turned upside down.

We touch a bead with a fingertip,
watch it vanish,
then wait for the next one to fall
because it always does.
The storm leaves us listening
for echoes stitched into the wood,
proof that the house holds rain
long after the sky moves on.

Autumn Shoes by the Door

They gather in a loose circle,

mud on the soles,

laces asking for patience.

Little pairs become less little,

sandals slide back,

boots step forward.

Leaves hitchhike in on treads,

carry the yard into the hallway.

The mat accepts every visitor,

the expected and the wild.

We choose footwear

like we choose our days,

what we are ready to face,

what we hope to avoid.

Rain speaks from the porch roof,

the umbrella makes its case again.

I kneel to tie a knot

on a boot that wants to run ahead.

The house steadies me

with a hand on the wall.

By night, the shoes rest.

They tell the mat what they learned.

The door listens,

its hinges quiet as breath.

Every year the circle shifts,

new sizes arriving,

old pairs fading into closets.

The house remembers them all.

Section V:
Inheritance and Continuance

Echoes in the Stairwell

The stairwell holds sound longer than it should.

Footsteps climb, pause, then fade,

but the air repeats them anyway,

as if unwilling to let go.

Children's voices once tangled there,

braids of laughter caught in the corners.

At night, a cough slipped upward,

bounced from railing to ceiling.

Even whispered arguments lingered,

their edges softened by wood.

Now the space feels emptier,

but when I pause halfway up,

I still hear the echo of weight.

The boards remember every footfall,

recording each rise and descent.

Sometimes I place my hand on the wall,

feel the hum beneath the paint.

It is not silence.

It is history rehearsing itself.

The stairwell keeps what we forget to hold.

The Walls Remember What We Forget

We misplace details.

Keys. Birthdays. Promises

made in the rush between errands.

The walls do not.

They recall the exact pitch of crying

the night the fever broke.

They know which window cracked first,

which doorframe bore the pencil marks

that proved a body grew.

We forget the smell of sawdust

after the floor was repaired,

the sound of rain that year

it found a way inside.

The walls store it quietly,

retrieve it without judgment.

I walk through rooms

and think I am alone in memory,

but paint leans closer,

offering what I dropped.

A sigh, a shadow,

a name I meant to keep.

The walls hold it all

in compartments too deep for us.

They remember because someone must.

Every Room a Season

The nursery hummed with winter breath,

warmth rising against the frost.

The kitchen sang in spring,

pollen drifting through its open mouth.

Summer played loud upstairs,

games echoing across the floor.

Autumn curled in the den,

lamplight steady as leaves slipped past.

Each room claimed a weather,

not just outside but within.

Even the basement had its season,

damp persistence of an endless rain.

When I walk the house now,

I feel the shift as I cross thresholds.

Rooms carry their seasons like coats,

hanging them on hooks for later use.

Some doors open into memory of snow,

others into heat thick with cicadas.

The house arranges the year for me,

a calendar written in wood and air.

Blueprint of Our Days

The blueprint was once clean lines,

angles exact,

rooms nameless but waiting.

Now the plan is smudged with living.

Walls bear fingerprints

in places no one imagined.

Floors bend a little,

accepting

weight that never stops arriving.

The dining room was supposed to be square.

Instead it is rounded with stories,

edges softened by laughter.

The hallway stretched longer

than the architect intended,

grown by years of footsteps,

by absence measured between visits.

I trace the paper sometimes,

see what was imagined.

Then I walk the rooms,

see what became.

No architect could have known

the mark of crayon beneath paint,

the hollow in a stair that learned our pace.

Blueprints are promises,

but the house writes its own plan,

every day another line

drawn in dust and breath.

The Yard Beyond the Fence

The yard is wide,

but the fence keeps its boundaries neat.

Still, beyond the posts and wire,

the world presses close.

Deer step out of shadow,

testing the grass with cautious mouths.

Foxes leave tracks that vanish by noon.

The neighbor's maple leans over

as if to listen to our meals.

Children kick balls against the fence,

watch them bounce back,

a rule enforced by wood.

Sometimes they climb anyway,

learning the shape of trespass.

Windows record each crossing.

They know fences are only half-truths,

lines meant for comfort,

never permanence.

One day the yard will change hands,

the fence will gray,

the posts loosen.

Still the land will remember

a time when children believed

nothing waited beyond the gate.

Future Keys, Unknown Hands

The keys will not always be ours.

Metal remembers more hands

than we allow ourselves to imagine.

One day they will turn for strangers,

unlocking air that no longer belongs to us.

Drawers will be filled with other letters,

other crumbs will darken the counters.

A child will press a new crayon

into the wall,

and the mark will stay

beside the ghost of ours.

We think of permanence as ours to keep.

But walls already know

they will belong to others.

They wait patiently,

ready to teach their rooms again,

ready to become memory

for someone else's story.

The House as Witness

All along it was watching.

The first key turned,

the first laugh broke the still air,

the first night tested our courage.

The house carried each moment

like a stone in its pocket.

It bore the weight of seasons,

the thrum of children's voices,

the hush of illness behind a door.

It mapped our living,

folded and refolded in its beams.

Now I see it clearly:

stairs repeating our weight,

windows widening for light,

hinges confessing their strain.

Every nail a historian,

every floorboard a ledger.

We thought we built the house.

But the house built us,

story by story,

breath by breath.

It waits in silence,

patient and sure,

bearing what we could not.

It will outlast us,

keep its witness,

hold its testimony

in wood and dust,

in echoes that refuse silence,

long after our voices

have gone quiet.

Veronica Tucker is an emergency medicine and addiction medicine physician and poet living in New Hampshire. Her work explores the quiet intersections of care, memory, and home. When not writing or working in the hospital, she enjoys fitness, travel, and time with her husband and three children. The House as Witness is her first chapbook.